21st Century Skills **INNOVATION** *Library*

Soccer

by K. C. Kelley

Published in the United States of America by Cherry Lake Publishing
Ann Arbor, Michigan
www.cherrylakepublishing.com

Content Adviser: Thomas Sawyer, EdD, Professor of Recreation and Sport Management, Indiana
State University

Design: The Design Lab

Photo Credits: Cover and page 3, ©iStockphoto.com/jcyoung2; page 5, ©iStockphoto.
com/Grafissimo; page 7, ©iStockphoto.com/mikedabell; page 9, ©moodboard/Alamy; page
10, ©iStockphoto.com/JBryson; page 12, ©Joe Fox/Alamy; page 15, ©Sandro Donda, used
under license from Shutterstock, Inc.; page 17, ©Stephen Aaron Rees, used under license from
Shutterstock, Inc.; page 19, ©iStockphoto.com/fredrocko; page 20, ©iStockphoto.com/gchutka;
page 22, ©iStockphoto.com/StacyBeck; page 25, ©Rainer Raffalski/Alamy; page 26, ©Pictorial
Press Ltd/Alamy; page 27, ©AP Photo/Khue Bui; page 28, ©AP Photo/Eugene Hoshiko

Library of Congress Cataloging-in-Publication Data
Kelley, K. C.
Soccer / by K. C. Kelley.
    p. cm.–(Innovation in sports)
Includes index.
ISBN-13: 978-1-60279-261-6
ISBN-10: 1-60279-261-5
1. Soccer–Juvenile literature. I. Title. II. Series.
GV943.25.K45 2008
796.334–dc22   2008006749

Cherry Lake Publishing would like to acknowledge the work of
The Partnership for 21st Century Skills.
Please visit www.21stcenturyskills.org for more information.

CONTENTS

Chapter One
History of Soccer   4

Chapter Two
Developing the Rules   9

Chapter Three
Styles of Play   14

Chapter Four
Equipment   19

Chapter Five
Soccer's Great Innovators   24

Glossary   30
For More Information   31
Index   32
About the Author   32

CHAPTER ONE

History of Soccer

Games that involve kicking a ball have been played throughout the world for centuries. The Chinese began playing a game called *cuju* as early as the second and third centuries bce. The Romans played their own variation of a ball-kicking game called *harpastum*. These games evolved into the world's most popular sport—soccer!

Early ball-kicking games were usually very disorganized. In the British Isles, ball games with kicking and throwing were the most popular. The favorite of these games was football. By the mid-1800s, however, many players were becoming confused. Was the game of "football" played with the hands (carrying the ball) or with the feet (kicking it)? In 1863, a meeting was held at Freemasons' Tavern in London to solve the problem. Groups of players from each version of the sport

Soccer players cannot use their hands, so they often make incredible kicks to keep the ball in play.

gathered. The players decided to create two separate sports—rugby football (with the hands) and football (no hands).

Rugby football is still played around the world. It is especially popular in Australia. But football became even more popular than rugby. By 1904, football had spread to countries around the world, including the United States. Although the rest of the world calls the game football, Americans call the game soccer. Soccer is short for the game's original name, **association** football or "assoc."

In 1904, eight countries created the Fédération Internationale de Football Association (FIFA, pronounced FEE-fah). By 1930, FIFA had 40 members, including the United States. FIFA put on the first World Cup in 1930 as a championship among soccer nations. It was held in Uruguay and won by Uruguay! The World Cup is held every four years. Brazil has won the most World Cup championships—five.

Today, soccer is more than just the World Cup. Many nations have **professional** leagues. Those leagues each have annual champions. Top soccer players often split their time between their professional league clubs and their national teams. Some players leave their native lands to play pro soccer, but still play for their national teams.

In America, soccer is not nearly as big as it is in other countries, but its popularity is growing. An 11 year-old pro league called Major League Soccer (MLS) now has teams in 13 U.S. cities. The U.S. National Team is among the world's top 15 teams. The United States has also

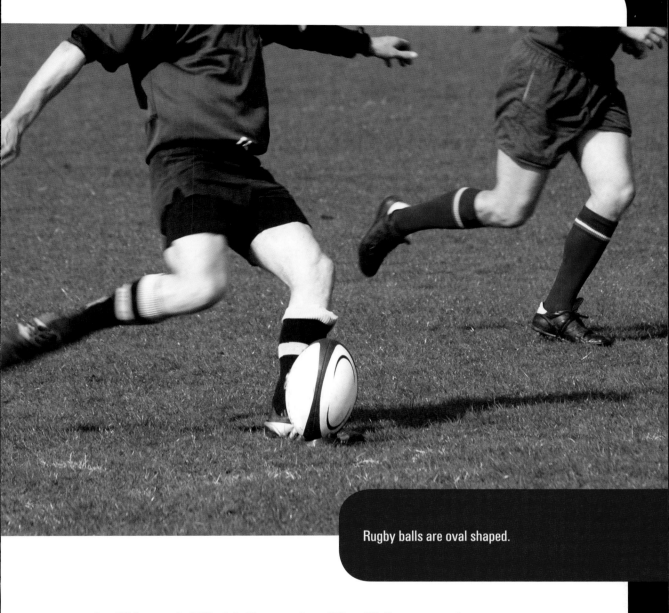

Rugby balls are oval shaped.

won the Women's World Cup twice. The U.S. women's team remains one of the most dominant teams in international competition.

21st Century Content

Soccer's popularity can play a role in bringing together people from different backgrounds. For example, France has citizens who come from all over the world. Sometimes this clash of backgrounds causes problems. But in 2006, that mixture caused joy. France's national soccer team advanced to the World Cup final. All of France cheered on a team in which 17 of the 23 players were from immigrant families. For fans, it no longer mattered if a player was black or white, Christian or Muslim. What mattered was that he played his heart out for France.

Satellite TV and the Internet have helped soccer grow in popularity. Today, TV viewers can watch games featuring the top teams in leagues from around the world. The Internet is also a rich source of soccer information. Fans can find highlight clips of their favorite players, videos of amazing goals, and all the latest info on pro and national teams.

More than a billion people watch the World Cup final. FIFA now has more than 200 countries as members. More people play soccer than any other sport. Soccer truly is the world's game!

CHAPTER TWO

Developing the Rules

Among major international sports, soccer is one of the easiest to understand. It has only a few rules, known as the "Laws of the Game." Unlike many other sports, these laws have not changed much over the years.

In a game, each team has 11 players. They move the ball back and forth among themselves, trying to get the ball into the opponent's goal. The goal is 8 yards (7.3 meters) wide and 8 feet (2.4 m) high. The object of the game is to score more goals than the opponent.

Players often "head" the ball, meaning they use their heads to make a pass or a shot on the goal.

The most obvious rule is that players can't use their hands or arms to control the ball. Only goalies may use their hands on the field, and only in the large "penalty area" in front of the goal. The top of that penalty box is 18 yards (16.5 m) from the goal line.

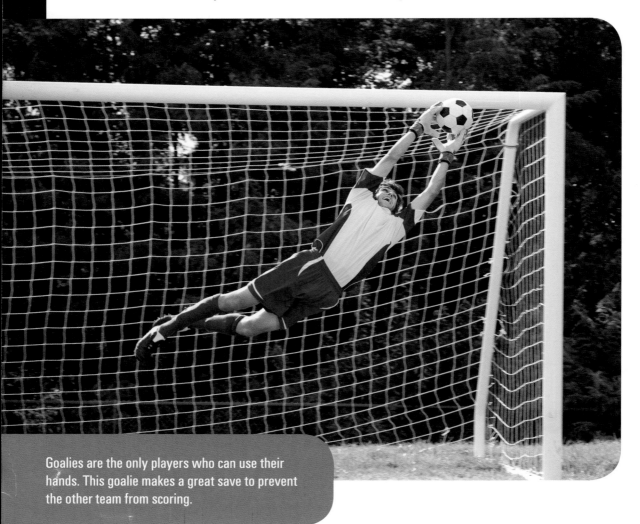

Goalies are the only players who can use their hands. This goalie makes a great save to prevent the other team from scoring.

Skilled players can trap or control the ball with their feet, knees, thighs, chest, and head. They can also make passes or shots with their head or feet. The great Brazilian player Ronaldinho made a stunning pass with his back in a 2007 game that led directly to a teammate's goal. Players pass the ball to their teammates, or advance it by **dribbling**. This is a great way to cover a lot of ground quickly. To dribble, players use small taps of their feet on the ball to get through opponents.

The most confusing rule in soccer is **offside** (not "offsides," as it is sometimes mistakenly called). It's been a part of the rules since that meeting back in 1863. The rule states that an offensive player must have two defensive players between himself and the goal when a ball is played forward toward him. One of those defenders is usually the goalie. Coaches and players had a problem with this rule. They thought that the rule prevented them from scoring more. As a result, the rule has been updated to make it clearer. FIFA has called for referees not to call a player offside if he or she is not "involved in the play." This has made the game much smoother and helped teams create more offense.

Another innovation was the introduction of red and yellow cards in the late 1960s. Up to that point, the referee would write, in a small notebook, the name of a player who committed a foul. You might still hear about

A referee will give a player a yellow card as a warning for fouling another player or for any inappropriate behavior.

players being "booked." But it wasn't always clear to fans and coaches why the ref booked a player. This was especially confusing in international play, when teams spoke different languages.

British referee Ken Ashton watched a World Cup game in which no one was sure why a player from Argentina had been kicked out of the game. On his way home, Ashton watched a traffic light turn yellow and then red. Bingo! He suggested that players be given a warning with a yellow card. Then fans, coaches, and other players will all know what's up. Getting two yellow cards equals a red card, and the player is kicked out of the game. Plus, the team cannot replace that player and must continue with only 10 on the field. A referee can give a red card right away for a very serious or dangerous foul.

Watching the best players in the world compete is amazing. Soccer players have to be not only great athletes, but also mindful of the rules. Fans know that these skills make soccer "the beautiful game" that it is today.

Life & Career Skills

Players work their way up from youth leagues to get to the top level. It is no different for referees. Referees will tell you that keeping an eye on all the players and the rules is a tough job. Like the players, it takes a lot of training to become a referee. First, you have to learn the rules thoroughly. Then you have to work with more experienced officials to improve your skills. You also have to stay in good shape. Referees work their way up from school games to college games to pro leagues. Only the very best referees from around the world get to work at the top level. But they all started out blowing their whistle for games with little kids!

CHAPTER THREE

Styles of Play

All soccer teams play by the same rules, but some teams have developed different styles of play. Teams use different **formations** on the field. A formation is how players are arranged on the field by the coach. During a game, players might find themselves anywhere on the field. Depending on their position, players are always responsible for their assigned area.

There are four main positions in most formations: goalie, defenders, **midfielders**, and forwards. The goalie always guards the goal. Aside from the goalie, there are dozens of formation combinations. A team or a coach will choose a formation based on the style of play he wants. A formation with many defenders is designed to stop goals, not score them. A formation with a big forward line is hoping to outscore the other team, instead

Every soccer team has its own style of play.

of stopping the other team from scoring. The midfield can be used to add to both offense and defense.

One successful formation used in soccer's early days focused on offense. The pyramid, or 2-3-5, included a wide forward line to cover the whole field. (In soccer formations, the numbers start from the back and refer to how many players are in each section. In the 2-3-5 formation, there are two defenders, three **midfielders**, and five forwards. The goalie is not included in formation numbers.) Uruguay used this formation to win the first World Cup in 1930.

Sometimes, innovation in sports means coming up with ideas that work for your particular team. A 4-2-4 formation was used by Brazil in the 1950s and 1960s. Brazil won three World Cups during that time. Brazil's formation was full of flair and ball control, which were the team's strengths. The formation was nicely balanced between offense and defense.

The most popular formation today is the 4-4-2. This formation divides the four midfielders equally on offense and defense. They provide "links" between the back and the front of the formation. Some teams today use a version called 3-6-1, which packs more players in the midfield, with a lone "striker" up front.

These formations show how teams start play and move around the field. They don't show the ways that

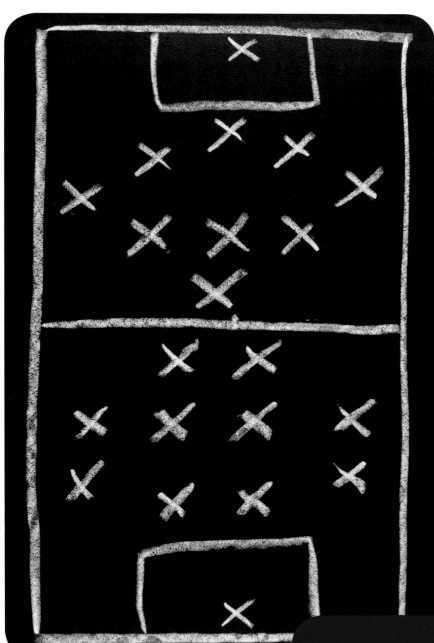

Different teams have different formations. This diagram shows 5-3-1 (top) and 4-4-2 (bottom).

Learning & Innovation Skills

The search for the perfect soccer formation continues. As players become faster, some teams are trying to find ways to get them room to run. Taller players are coming into the game, too. Their spot in the central defense can cause problems for offenses. Coaches constantly tinker with their lineups to get the best players in the right spots. If you were putting a team together with your friends, what formation would you use? How would you arrange your team to make the best formation?

teams move the ball around. Three styles of soccer have evolved over time as teams tried out new moves on the playing field. Each style is associated with a country. The English style is more physical and uses more tackling. Players are more likely to make a long pass forward and have people run to it. The Brazilian style uses many short passes and lots of dribbling. It focuses much more on individual play and can be very entertaining to watch. The Italian style is very defensive. In fact, they call soccer *calico*, which means "wall." They try to score, but they focus more on defense.

Some nations use parts of these general styles of play. German soccer takes parts of the English and Italian games, and adds a very organized strategy of play. Most South American teams use a Brazilian-style game of flash and flair. These are not rules, just overall forms of how teams play. All teams, no matter what style or formation, always aim to win!

CHAPTER FOUR

Equipment

ost professional soccer games are played on grass. Grass fields require a lot of maintenance, money, and time. They also wear out quite easily. Not every school or park can afford to take care of its field. This problem was solved in the 1990s, when a new kind of surface called FieldTurf was created by a Montreal-based company. FieldTurf is a plastic mat with many individual stalks, like grass, that is laid out over a surface. Then a

Grass soccer fields can require a lot of maintenance.

Soccer balls have been redesigned over the years. And today, most players wear cleats during a game.

huge amount of small rubber pellets is poured over the stalks. This fills in the spaces and creates a flat, true-bouncing surface. It is easily cared for and can withstand many games without wearing down. Also, FieldTurf's soft surface can prevent many injuries that occur when playing on artificial turf.

Soccer balls vary in size, depending on the age of the players. Smaller, lighter balls are used for many youth leagues. Adult- or professional-sized balls are used for older players.

In the beginning, the ball was a heavy, leather **sphere**. The ball sometimes had exposed laces holding the pieces of leather together. Inside the leather was a rubber "bladder" that held the air. During play, the leather covering would become wet and even heavier. Also, balls would lose their round shape throughout the game.

Soccer balls didn't change dramatically until after World War II. New techniques for making rubber meant that the bladders were sturdier. Ball makers added a layer of cloth around the bladder and under the leather. This helped balls stay round. Water-resistant coatings invented during the war years helped the ball keep from becoming waterlogged.

Today, millions of dollars are spent on soccer ball research. Using computer modeling, companies create patterns of leather pieces that help the ball move through the air even more smoothly.

You can play soccer in your sneakers (or in your bare feet at the beach), but players usually wear cleats. Cleats have hard plastic soles with short studs sticking out from the bottom. These studs help the player get a good grip on the ground.

The first soccer shoes looked more like heavy-duty, high-top basketball shoes. They went over the ankle. Their studs were made of leather and were much longer. In the 1920s, screw-in studs were made by Adi Dassler of the adidas company. For the first time, players could choose the length of studs that was right for the type of field they were on. Playing on a muddy field? Use longer cleats. What about a dry, dusty field? Try the smaller ones. By the 1950s, the invention of plastics allowed cleat-covered soles to be made of one molded piece per shoe. Top players sometimes still use screw-ins, but most players now wear molded cleats.

To avoid injury, most players wear shin guards under their soccer socks.

Another innovation is the placement of the laces. On some shoes, the laces are set to the inside of the foot, instead of in the middle. This gives the kicker a flatter surface to strike the ball. Some expert players can use these shoes to give their kicks extra spin to get around opponents.

Soccer players also wear shin guards. These protect the front of the leg from accidental kicks. Goalies can wear thick, padded gloves to help them catch shots that can go more than 70 miles (113 kilometers) per hour. No matter what kind of player you are, having the right equipment is important for safety and fun.

21st Century Content

Some soccer cleats are made from kangaroo leather. In 2007, when British star David Beckham joined the Los Angeles Galaxy, controversy arose about the use of these animals. Beckham wore a brand of shoe called the Predator that was usually made from kangaroos. The state of California tried to ban the sale of all shoes made from kangaroo leather. Many people said that Australians should not be killing the animals. The Australian government and the shoemaker, adidas, said they were not killing any endangered species. Kangaroos, they said, were plentiful.

Because of the controversy, Beckham said that his soccer "boots" would only be made from fake leather, not leather made from kangaroo skins. The controversy is not over. Many people still object to using kangaroos to make soccer shoes.

CHAPTER FIVE

Soccer's Great Innovators

Many people have had an impact on the growth of soccer over the years. Some were leaders off the field, helping to bring the game to new countries and fans. Others changed the game on the field, through their play or their personality. Let's meet several innovators who had a big effect on the game of soccer.

Jules Rimet

In 1921, this Frenchman was named president of FIFA. At the time, the organization had about two dozen member countries. By the time he retired 33 years later, FIFA had grown more than three times as large. Soccer had become the world's number-one sport. Rimet started the World Cup in 1930, giving world soccer a stage for its international championship. Today, the World Cup is

These Brazilian fans celebrate a World Cup win in a 2006 match against Ghana. Jules Rimet started the World Cup in 1930.

the largest sporting event on Earth. An audience of more than 33 billion watched all or part of the 27 days of the 2006 World Cup. Rimet's leadership helped establish soccer as a global game.

Pelé

Born Edson Arantes do Nascimento, Pelé got his famous nickname as a boy in Brazil. He played in the streets, wearing no shoes and using a sock or rags for a ball. He later helped the Brazil National Team win three World Cups (1958, 1962, and 1970). In 1975, he came to the United States to play for the New York Cosmos.

Pelé is one of the best-known names in soccer. His star status helped promote the sport.

He helped ignite an interest in soccer in the United States that is still growing today. His total of 1,280 goals is unmatched by any current player. Pelé's always-bright personality made people love the game of soccer. He showed how much he loved the game by how he played. And he showed how much he loved people by how he smiled.

Mia Hamm

For most of soccer's history, women went unnoticed. Few women played the game, and never at a top international level. That all changed in the 1990s, when women finally got their own World Cup. Leading the way was Mia Hamm, who had joined the U.S. National Team at the age of 15 in 1987. She later helped the University of North Carolina win four national college titles.

Mia Hamm (left) holds the record for the most goals scored in international play.

Led by Hamm, the United States won the first Women's World Cup in 1991. The victory helped soccer boom in the United States, especially among young girls. Mia was their hero. Over the years, she added a 1999 World Cup title and two Olympic gold medals to her record. She also scored 158 goals in international play, a record among men and women. Hamm was elected to the National Soccer Hall of Fame in 2007.

David Beckham, shown here with a group of kids in China, was captain of England's national team before moving to Los Angeles, California.

David Beckham

David Beckham is one of the most recognizable athletes on the planet today. He first hit the international stage in 1995, when he became a starter for the Manchester United professional team. His instant success landed him a position on England's national football team as captain. He has appeared in three World Cups with England (1998, 2002, 2006).

Beckham made a splash in 2007 when he signed a contract with MLS's Los Angeles Galaxy. He is a strong midfielder with unique ball-handling and passing abilities. He is known mostly for his dramatic flair in kicking free kicks. Beckham's free kicks bend in midair around defenders, easily scoring goals. Many soccer players today try to "bend it like Beckham."

Glossary

association (uh-soh-see-AY-shuhn) a gathering of similar individuals or groups

clash (KLASH) a disagreement or conflict

dribbling (DRIB-ling) in soccer, a way to control the ball by using small taps of the feet

formations (for-MAY-shuhnz) ways of organizing players on a soccer field

midfielders (mid-FEELD-uhrz) players in the center of the field who play both offense and defense

offside (OFF-side) a rule in soccer that says an offensive player must have two defensive players between himself and the goal when a ball is played toward him

professional (pruh-FESH-uh-nuhl) a person who performs a job or plays a sport for money

sphere (SFIHR) a ball- or globe-shaped object

For More Information

BOOKS

Beckham, David. *David Beckham's Soccer Skills*. New York: Harper Collins, 2007.

Buckley, James. *Soccer Superstars*. Mankato, MN: Child's World, 2006.

Cline-Ransome, Lesa. *Young Pelé: Soccer's First Star*. New York: Schwartz & Wade, 2007.

Soccer: Eyewitness Books. New York: DK Publishing, 2005.

WEB SITES

American Youth Soccer Organization (AYSO)
www.soccer.org
The home page of the nationwide nonprofit youth soccer organization

FIFA
www.fifa.com
The site of world soccer's organizing group

Major League Soccer
www.mlsnet.com
Home page of the top U.S. pro soccer league

Index

Ashton, Ken, 13
association football, 6

Beckham, David, 23, 29
"booking," 12
Brazilian style, 18

cleats, 21–22, 23
coaches, 11, 12, 14, 18
computers, 21
control, 11

Dassler, Adi, 22
defenders, 14, 16
dribbling, 11

English style, 18

Fédération Internationale
  de Football Association
  (FIFA), 6, 8, 11, 24
fields, 19–20
FieldTurf, 19–20
football, 4, 5, 6
formations, 14, 16, 18

forwards, 14, 16
fouls, 11–12
Freemasons' Tavern, 4–5

German style, 18
gloves, 23
goalies, 10, 11, 14, 16,
  23
goals, 8, 9, 10, 11, 14,
  26, 28

Hamm, Mia, 27–28

injuries, 20
Internet, 8
Italian style, 18

kangaroos, 23

laces, 23
Laws of the Game, 9
leagues, 6, 8, 13, 21
Los Angeles Galaxy,
  23, 29

Major League Soccer
  (MLS), 6, 29
Manchester United, 29
midfielders, 14, 16

national teams, 6–7,
  25, 27
New York Cosmos, 25

offside rule, 11
Olympic Games, 28
origins, 4–6

passes, 11
Pelé, 25–26
penalty box, 10
physical fitness, 13
positions, 14
Predator shoe, 23
pyramid formation, 16

red cards, 11–12, 13
referees, 11, 13
Rimet, Jules, 24–25
RoboCup, 29

Ronaldinho, 11
rugby football, 5, 6
rules, 9, 10, 11, 13

satellite television, 8
shin guards, 23
shoes, 21–23
shots, 11, 23
soccer balls, 21
strikers, 16
styles, 18

U.S. National Team, 6–7

Women's World Cup
  championship, 7, 27,
  28
World Cup champion-
  ship, 6, 7, 8, 13, 16,
  24–25, 29

yellow cards, 11–12, 13
youth leagues, 13

About the Author

K. C. Kelley has written many books and magazine articles about sports for young readers. He has played soccer since he was seven years old (he still plays on an over-30 team!) and has coached kids' soccer, too. One of his favorite sports memories was attending several games at the 1994 World Cup in Los Angeles.